Laurine's inspirations (and the lovely artwork) transported me to a better world... and somehow, a part of me is still there!

—Denis Ouellette, www.NaturalLifeNews.com

The majesty of the mountains, the pressing flow of ice-fed rivers, and the brave flowers that carry the soul of Montana find their expression in Laurine's poetry. This is a wonderful collection to take with you on a hike, a camping trip, a walk in the country and by reading, to hear what nature, in her Power, her Wisdom, and her Love, would teach you.

—Eleanor Rosenzweig, LCSW

May this little volume of verses accomplish God's purpose and draw its readers to truth, love and joy!

—Theresa Thomas

When I read Laurine's poems, I sense a resonance with the devotional work of the late Paramahansa Yogananda. Like this great master, Laurine draws readers right into her rich spiritual life. Skillfully weaving the personal with the universal, these poems show us a path beyond limiting beliefs. If we allow ourselves to become immersed in their crisp imagery, the poems lead us to an experience of oneness with all that is.

I recognize Laurine as a present-day mystic. May you savor these gifts from her heart.

—Marie Mally Lynn, MA, Author of "Like Father, Like Daughter: A Memoir across Time"

A beautiful vision of the world of true being... *Wow!*
—*Jeffrey Lewis, Voice Dialogue Therapist*

From the beginning of the book, Laurine invites the reader on a journey full of Wisdom, Love, and Power. The section divisions act as a guide to help you find the poems you subconsciously need. The opening poem of the book, "I Am One," is a mantra the reader takes with them through the journey of *Kisses from the Wind*, and I found its meter driving the experience.

In "The Small Inner Voice," Laurine writes about how important it is to stop mental chatter. This poem, grouped in the Power section of the book, shows the cyclical characteristics of Laurine's writing. This wisdom, toward the end of the book, helps the reader reflect upon the Wisdom with which the book began.
—*Ashley Margaret Waterman, MFA, Writing & Poetics*

The tender poems in *Kisses from the Wind* are also comforting prayers and affirmations—joyful reminders that at any point on our path, we can rekindle our heart's longing to celebrate and touch the light that is within and around us.
—*Patricia Spadaro, Author of "Honor Yourself: The Inner Art of Giving and Receiving"*

Colorful and radiant word images remind us to spend time with what is real and beautiful—and what is hidden deep within.
—*Victoria Lewis, spiritual counselor*

Kisses from the Wind

LOVE
POEMS
AND
RHAPSODIES
FROM
MY HEART
TO
YOURS

Laurine Perla McMahon

Illustrations by Misty Taylor

Caldera
PUBLISHERS

Kisses from the Wind
*Love Poems and Rhapsodies
from My Heart to Yours*

Laurine Perla McMahon
Illustrations by Misty Taylor

Copyright © 2014 by Laurine McMahon & Caldera Publishers

All rights reserved. No part of this publication may be reproduced or utilized in any form by any means, electronic or mechanical, including photocopying, recording, or by any information storage or retrieval system, without permission in writing from the publisher.

ISBN 978-0692274880 (print)

1. Poetry
2. Spirituality

More information and additional copies from

Caldera Publishers
1106 West Park Street, #137
Livingston, Montana 59047

Available through Amazon.com

Printed in the United States of America

DEDICATED

To all who honor the Good,
To all who seek the highest Wisdom,
To all who desire to be of benefit to the Whole,
And to the Great Mother.

ACKNOWLEDGMENTS

I would like to give special thanks to my true sister of light, Misty Taylor, whose beautiful illustrations have captured the tone and essence of these poems so exquisitely.

I am grateful to Denis Ouellette, my editor and layout artist, for his patience and mentoring. His expertise has been invaluable to me as a first-time self-publisher. He is also a special heartfriend and seeker of truth.

I also want to thank Jeffrey, my beloved soul mate, whose magnanimous love and wisdom permeate my life. He worked alongside Denis in art direction, editing and layout.

I give thanks for my parents who made this life possible; also, my wonderful sisters Suzanne, Joanne and Wendy and my brother Everett, who gave my heart a purpose and focus from the early years.

I also want to thank my childhood teacher, Grace Reinhart, who came from Newcomers Town, Ohio to Lima, Montana. She inspired me to look for and become a 'beautiful dreamer.'

I credit my teachers both old and new: Gautama Buddha, St. Bonaventure, Plato, Plotinus, and Ken Wilbur, the contemporary researcher of comparative spiritual traditions and philosopher of modern science.

To my beloved teacher and friend, Candice, a true diamond being, whose fierce, adamantine awareness showed me where it all comes together and makes sense.

PREFACE

Dear Reader,

My desire is that this outpouring will encourage, benefit and delight, support, and comfort you. Many of these poems were written to particular people with these ends in mind; yet, the universality of the issues and their resolution are meant for all.

Other poems have come while resting in the heart flame and the true nature of mind. I can take little credit for the flow of light or for the transcendent visions which emerged. The poems' words are the crystalization of these energies.

While I have used certain figures of speech to indicate the core identity—the Presence, Inner Light, the One, or the Good— there are as many names for the divine as there are cultures. As one of my favorite teachers once said, "God does not care what you call him—just so you do make the call."

The clarity and light that comes from attunement with our inner being allowed these *Kisses from the Wind* to be released, like a butterfly from its cocoon.

I hope you enjoy them!
Laurine

CONTENTS

WISDOM

I Am One 11
My Heart Is Burning 12
Jenny Lake Muses 13
Upon This Land 14
Glad Shouts 15
The Sacred Tryst 16
Cherished Delight 18
A Flash of Intuition 19
Wishing for You 20
Notes to Myself... 21
Celebration 22
Soul of Light 23
Affirmations for My Sisters 24
Love Divine 26
What You Desire 27
Watering My Tree 29
Burning Ember 30

LOVE

Hearts of Roses 35
A True Teacher 36
Love Notes to... 37
Hold You Tight 38
Rose of Sharon 39
A Day Like Today 40

Hooray! 41
This Miraculous Fact of Life 42
Wonder of Wonders 44
A Mighty Heart 45
Jenny Lake Haikus 46
The Holy Spirit 47
Evening Prayer 48
How Great My Longing! 51
To Feel One 52

POWER

Open the Storehouse .57
Morning Prayer 58
Sparkling Gem 59
Threefold Flame 60
Hand in Hand 62
What's Out and About 63
The Waiting Shakti Saga 64
Let All Who Would Follow 66
Scintillating Ray 68
Rest Deep Inside 70
The Small Inner Voice 71
Most Dear 72
Great Spirit I AM 73
Put Your Arms Around Me 77
The Touchstone 78

WISDOM

I Am One

I Am One.
I Am One.
I Am One.
With my Father, with my Mother, I Am one.
O luminous Presence of Life, I Am one.

I Am a dazzling, radiant, yellow-white sun.
I Am this shining—oh, it is fun.

I Am one, I Am one, I Am one.
I Am this light—of the Great Central Sun!

Now that I'm shining in all that I've done
The Presence of light is victory won.

We are One, we are One—we are The One!

My Heart Is Burning

My heart is burning;
There is a coal within—

A burning ember,
Which to my soul is kin.

For, it is this fire,
With its heartfelt desire,

Fully loaded and coiled
And recently oiled.

It spirals out in great love
Inspired by harmony's dove,

A beacon to all souls
Becoming the fire within!

Jenny Lake Muses

Sun, shooting down canyons—
Water laps.

Oh, I wish I could see
How close I am to reaching Thee.

The trees rising up, their tops like spires
Like me they're aspiring;
To be tall as can be, and to reach up to Thee.

Upon This Land

Upon this land,
    by the work of our hand,
We stamped our vision,
    joy and love.

With mindful hearts
    we did our part
        to bring down heaven above.

The plants we knew,
    which spaces they grew,
All came from our Holy Dove.

So enjoy this elm,
    know who's at the helm,
And follow your heart
    to the source of all love!

Glad Shouts

Beloved friends of light and grace,
How I long to see your face,

On this day to wake up
Where the sky's always blue
And be face-to-face
With hearts so true.
Knowing this moment
Always already, a part of you.

Today on my birthday
My heart cries out—
My glad longing for you
Inspires my shout!

The Sacred Tryst

O Mighty God,
O Mighty God within,

Still my outer vehicles,
Shut out the worldly din.

Take all my thoughts and energies,
Subdue them with Thy voice!

In Thy shining clarity
Make clear the higher choice!

Then I join the sacred tryst—
A meeting so sublime

My heart and hand, I offer you
Whate'er I thought was mine.

My name and fame, my contacts of the earth,
Surrendered all for that of eternal worth.

Rejoicing in this moment
Thy fire infusing mine.

Now, in our wedding chamber
With splendor shining bright,

In Thy majestic presence
Our two-in-one, unite!

Cherished Delight

O radiant One of glorious light,
The touchstone on high of heaven's might.

Even in this plane of densest plight,
Our hearts ray out to fulfill Thy sight.

For in this journey of darkest night,
Thy love and light is our cherished delight!

A Flash of Intuition

The first snow falls,
    some leaves still intact,
    to let us know—soon,
    we'll start a new act.

Months turn to years—
    cycles come and go.

All so apparent,
    seen in a flash,
    as the snowflakes fell
    and we had to dash.

Wishing for You

Ahhhhhh—my dear friend,

In the meditative cycle of life,
Free from the clutter
And all outer strife.

We wait through the years,
Shedding not a few tears,
To come to the place
Where we've conquered our fears.

So here is my love,
And my song just for you.

Wishing all the strands of your melody
Come together and set your life free.

Notes to Myself...

Hallelujah!
My God is near.
Right inside,
I know He's here!

Wherever I wander,
Wherever I roam,
You are in my heart
that is my home!

O light of God, I Am divine
Take all I do and make it Thine.
By going within and reaching way up,
Offering my heart as your betrothed,
I have made you my daily cup.

O Hooray! Glorious day!
When I am one with You.

Celebration

Oh, light of my heart,
Gift to my soul,
I'm doing my part—
Now make me whole.

My attention's on thee,
Forsaking all else.
What's important to me
Is my only True Self.

I honor thy flame;
I bathe in each plume.
No longer the same,
I am cleaning each room.

Hidden light of my soul,
Yellow, pink and blue,
Making pearls for God—
Rising up unto you.

The pearl is returned
From my Presence on high,
Know what I've learned?
My wholeness is nigh.

I am grateful to God.
His messengers, too.
My own Flaming Yod,
I am adoring you!

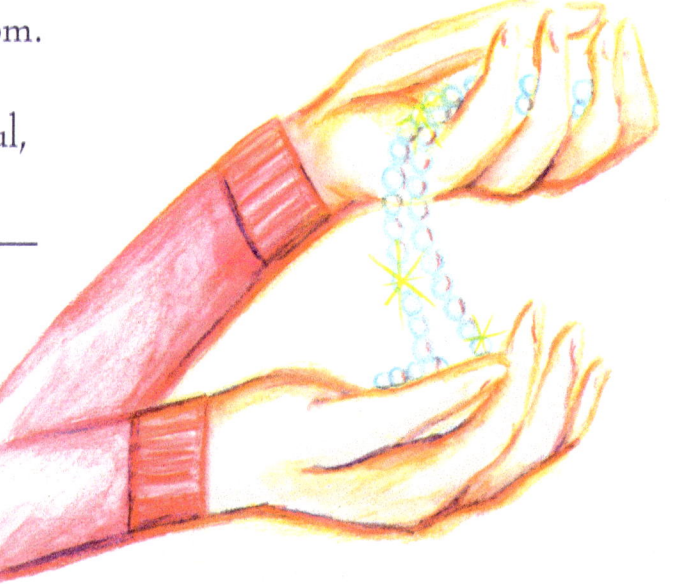

Soul of Light

O soul of light,
In trying your best
To reach heaven's height,

To mirror the image—
above and inside,
To let the pain
Dissolve and subside.

You are working to create
the man, anew
No more facades,
just truly you,

With a breast full of love
for all that is,
As wisdom guides
Your heart's cortege.

And each day its own
'projet monumental'
Life—a miracle on earth,
Footsteps to the all!

Affirmations for My Sisters

I Am a divine being
   clothed in the soft curves of womanhood.

I Am filled with light and grace
   which radiates out to all.

I Am the love of the Creator for Her creation.

I Am the love of the creation for her Creator,
   and I am loving all of creation.

I Am now the fullness of all that I am,
   sharing that fullness with all life.

I Am manifesting abundance in the circle of my life,
I Am expanding the circle of abundance outward.

I Am the generous flow of abundance
   in all circles of life everywhere!

I stand in the fire of the emerald flame of abundance!

Love Divine

My beloved God Flame
And Christ Presence dear,
Fill my heart and mind today;
Give me vision clear.
By the Power of Love Divine
Embracing, drawing near.

O beloved God Flame,
By Thy Power and Grace
Swell and spin within me,
Radiance shining through my face,
Let the Wisdom of Love Divine
Transmit to all within my space.

And again, Dear God Flame
For Thee I make the case—
All other thoughts and feelings
Dissolve in purest space.
With my love, O Love Divine,
I want to win your grace!

What You Desire

O Mighty God I Am,
    Developed by your grace.
Through many incarnations here.
    Finally, I see your face.

The days so long
    The nights so short—
I realize I'm waiting
    To exit this place.

What can I do?
    Where should I be?
To finish what you
    Have slated for me?

What should I do?
    Where can I be?
To find meaning and give of myself
    Into the all of Thee?

The questions remain,
    My heart is on fire
To be, do and see—
    Only what You desire!

Watering My Tree

Lovely tripartite Light
Yellow, pink, blue
Holy gift from my Father
To you I'll be true.

Balance, blaze and expand
Throughout this form of mine
Filling all my aura
That's the plan divine.

Daily in devotions,
Spending time with Thee,
With attention and love,
like watering a tree,
Who'd ever think
I'd be watering me!

As I grow and I grow,
This fullness is planned
To unfurl the plumes
and blaze through this land.

Burning Ember

Burning ember within my heart,
Light of my days, you do impart,

Everything beautiful, flows from inside,
In this burning chamber, thy love abides.

O loving light of the majestic sun,
It's your love flowing, that gets the job done.

Magnanimous heart, abiding within,
All of thy names, are my potential to win.

Luminous light of the radiant gem,
Outshining all, I aspire and ascend!

LOVE

Hearts of Roses

Hearts of roses,
    fill our auras
With the wonders
    of your love.

Hearts of wonder,
    in gentle thunder
Sent through the aura
    filled with love.

Love flowing
    in a figure-eight tai chi,
Hearts, roses, auras,
    from Thee to me—
And me to Thee!

A True Teacher

The timeless heart, unborn, appears again
   as luminous essence, a spiritual friend.

But hidden from the merely casual view,
   her sword is sharpened and will cut through.

The radiant sun shines through her eyes
   and those who care offer their skies.

For her potent light, emanating out,
   will give to all—even those with doubt—

A crystal-clear lens, circular and true,
   and a lovefest of benefits displayed for you.

Love Notes to...

From the shores of Titicaca
    to the depths of human lore,
The beauty of your flaming shines
    as in many days of yore.

        Clear as crystal
           and the bluest expanse of sky
        Your words, a pure transmission
           delight the ear, and I.

To the Heart
    of the Eternal One
I send warm, loving wishes
    until this job is done.

        After the day is done,
           and all the songs are sung,
        I lie and wait for You
           to show me what to do.

Rose of Sharon

Roses are lovely,
Sweet-smelling, bright.
Oh, how holy is
Our bright inner light!

The more that we love you,
The more time we spend
loving, adoring, each petal unfolding,
More our own Rose of Sharon
Will be all a'glowing!

Hold You Tight

May your heart sing its song loud and clear
Even without crowds or persons to cheer.

The inner small voice is all that you need
For there you will find, for this life, your creed.

Be happy, be joyous—give all that you can—
Love and compassion 'boomerang and pan.'

So laugh through your days;
Sing through your nights—
Your Inner Self,
Will be holding you tight.

A Day Like Today

Embraced in the heart
   of the Divine One,
Guided, directed
   from the start,
We come here and play
   our royal part.

Stories unfold,
   eons go by
And here we still sit
   with our eye on the sky.

Then out of the blue
   and love's mist's golden hue
Comes a day like today
   with roses for you.

Hooray!

Delight of my eyes, pulse of my heart,
Another cycle with you as all cares depart.

The years we've been through and all we have seen
Are nothing to compare, with fulfillment of dreams.

Rejoice! Come what may we'll live out our days,
With stars from the sky lighting our way.

Leaving crystalline patterns to mark each, *hooray!*

This Miraculous Fact of Life

Life as one in all its sobs and glory,
Gives meaning to each day
   as we write our untold story.

Hours and days go by as untimed cycles unfold,
To each moment is given the movement,
   the guidance, until the body lies cold.

No sorrow remains untouched
   by this miraculous fact of life;
Gloriously tinged, the bud unfolds,
   revealing the truth—no strife!

Wonder of Wonders

O Wonder of Wonders,
You've beckoned me!
How is it so many people see?

Is it—Your radiance flowing?
Or maybe—my dedication showing?
Or perhaps—it's their soul knowing?

All is there, to see.
My reason for being—
Your crown to receive!
Though it's called 'my ascension'
It's Your Victory achieved.

A Mighty Heart

A mighty heart you have indeed—
A mighty heart—and all else you need.

For in that heart is a greatness seed.
As you grow up, it will spread good deeds.

So love the todays, practicing your art,
Victory surely will come to your mighty heart.

Lots of hugs and pure space will play their part
To unleash the torrent of your mighty heart.

Jenny Lake Haikus

Listen,
as the cathedrals
hear my heart.

                                            Quiet
                                            from the cathedrals
                                            stills the mind.

        Lake freshened body
        smoothed
        by a breeze.

                                              Cloud
                                            hiding the sun
                                            too soon gone.

The Holy Spirit

The Holy Spirit cometh like the leaves of a determined tree.
The Holy Spirit streameth as love between me and thee.

The Holy Spirit blesses the wonder of our destiny.
The Holy Spirit knows how we hone our capacity.

The Holy Spirit rejoices as we charge through adversity.
The Holy Spirit welcomes our nearness to victory!

Evening Prayer

O infinite all-pervading Presence,
Quickening the flame within my heart,
I give thanks for this day as it departs.

Honoring and loving each moment I see.
Thank you for all you have given me.

Show me tonight with great delight,
The next steps on this pathway of light.

O Great God Flame I Am,
Hold me tight.
Guide my days;
Embrace me all night!

How Great My Longing!

My beautiful radiant I Am Presence,
Author of my soul,
Take all distractions from me
Save devotion to Thy everpresent whole.

The words that stream together
In this precious time with Thee,
Are markings for my soul
Traveling on the infinite sea.

How long has been the journey
Through the vantage point of time.
Just how great my longing—
To unite with Thee, sublime!

O Love that pulls me upward,
Racing to the climb
Of mountains, steps and stairways
To embrace Thy Face Divine.

O wondrous, constant Presence,
Let me love you more today
Let all my hopes and yearnings
Meld into one great heart bouquet.

To Feel One

Glorious Radiant Presence,
    Thou God of me above,
How precious are the moments
    When I feel you with my love.

The days so long and boisterous
    Permit short moments now and then—
Retreats to inner sanctitude
    Allow all pains to mend.

Knowing in the quietude,
    I am this selfsame light.
Yet only in short moments
    Do I feel this truth so bright.

And in the evening dark
    With stillness all about,
Always and already,
    there can be no doubt.

There I rest in clarity
    To find the voice within,
As longer moments afford my love
    Sight and songs to heal the din.

To feel one—
    To feel one—
        Is to win!

POWER

Open the Storehouse

O love delight
    from heaven's height,
Fill my atoms, cells, electrons
    my seven chakras, too,
With all abundant mightiness
    I may receive from you.

Surround them each
    with a donut of pink;
Sound the tones
    to put me in sync!

Please fulfill divine intentions
    in this, my form, today.
Let Thy power and momentums
    always have their loving sway.

Open the storehouse!
    Let it rain down—
A Niagara Falls flowing
    through my vehicles redound!

Make haste, make haste;
    I'll shed not a tear,
Acceleration and perseverance.
    You are so near!

Morning Prayer

O Great God Flame,
    the heart of eternity,
Radiate Thy light
    that all may truly see.
Infusing Thy power
    throughout the form of me.

Release Thy heartfelt plan,
    for this very day
I, in execution—will do
    all I surely may.
Add your momentum;
    we will be winning all the way.

Thank you, I love you,
    Great God Flame
        I Am!

Sparkling Gem

Beloved ceaseless crystal stream,
Thou gift of God to all,
Quicken our perception of,
Your handwriting on the wall.

The light is streaming everywhere—
The signs are plain to see,
Thy beauty and thy majesty
Reveal yourself to me.

In daily comings and goings
Your touch is always there,
And in those special moments
I can only stop and stare!

Perceiving in this casual mix,
The rarest sparkling gem—
The timeless shining brilliance
Of all that's ever been!

It heightens all my senses—
Yes, you are truly there!

Threefold Flame

I Am your Threefold Flame;
    I am so very small
But if you'll spend some time with me,
    I'll grow up very tall.

I Am your Threefold Flame;
    I have begun to grow
Because you're spending time with me,
    I have made you glow.

I Am your Threefold Flame;
    I'm yellow, pink and blue
Now I am a little bigger—
    With your devotion through and through.

I Am your Threefold Flame;
    Now, I'm almost big as you
With inspiration from my heart,
    You know the perfect thing to do.

I Am your Threefold Flame;
    I am bigger now than you
Because you've danced with me so well
    We are now not two.

I Am your Threefold Flame;
    Spinning fast, as does the sun
As we rise in flaming purity—
    Transcendence—we are One!

Hand in Hand

As the veil grows thinner
And the time is drawing nigh,
The days we have together
Are surely more sublime.

Our comings and our goings,
Throughout the year we find,
Our priceless potent moments
Are never left behind.

We graze the higher ethers;
We walk the razors edge,
Out to the farthest touch point
Upon the precipice ledge.

With arms embracing
And fingers entwining,
Taking our steps
with crystal-clarity shining.

Hand in hand, heart to heart,
Finishing the great work—
Our mission fulfilled—
As seen from the start!

What's Out and About

O Everpresent Living Flame,
Help me now to clearly see,
What is within my mortal veils
That must come out of me.

Show me now what offends Thee
And slows the pace of what's meant to be.
Help me as I walk through this land
Trying to keep myself in hand.

Inspire me each moment and day that goes by
To keep my gaze clear as the sky.
Then I will hear Your prompt from within—
For nothing but You will be inside my skin!

Then, oh glorious day!
We both give a shout—
For what's truly within
Is what's out and about!

The Waiting Shakti Saga

Now that I've finished
Cleaning each room,
What am I doing
Whilst waiting for *my June*?

What am I doing each day
And each hour,
To climb up the stairs
And reach the top tower?

All thoughts are not lofty,
Some actions are small
Yet in the grand scheme
Their input's not 'the all'.

The thing that I know
Who really I am
Is grander by far
Than this stuff in the can!

Who I am, it is true,
(The same is of you)
Is the vastness of skies
and garlands of gems.
We've done this before—
And had better ends!

But this time around,
For better or worse,
We're in the harness of karma
And have to rehearse.

Pure Space is our place
Pay homage we must—
Nothing else on this planet
Gives a clue what to trust.

So—in spite of five senses
And their report to our brains
All they report
Is mostly a pain!

The truth is inside
Secret chamber within,
And to hear that small voice:
"Rest, rest, from the din,
then you'll be within!"

This, I am saying—
This, I know it is true:
Oh, Great God Flame,
I am loving you.

Let All Who Would Follow

Now that I'm finished
Now that I'm free
What will I do
While waiting for Thee?

My heart is on fire
My sails are full blown—
Will you follow the pathway
Where flowers we've strewn?

Alert to the message
And prompts from within,
I follow the course—
Only the One, can win!

The orbit we're on,
A fast track at best,
Hanging on, holding on
Until the great Rest.

Knowing for certain
The direction is home,
The steps that we've taken
Are all marked and shown.

May all who would follow—
Follow your own inner Star,
Ascend to the One—
So near, yet so far.

Scintillating Ray

Hidden light of my heart
Pink, yellow, blue,
When I think of my God
I am thinking of you.

So tiny, so small,
(a fraction of an inch)
Yet upon you I depend—
You are my cinch.

A baby bird in my hand
Is vulnerable, small,
Its life is so fragile,
Too easy to fall.

And you're smaller by far,
Lovely tripartite light,
Yet, your brilliance shines on
Like the sun—day or night.

Scintillating ray
of the Great Solar Flame,
You're my source and my tie,
To the Great I AM Name.

You were ignited in me,
With the first breath I drew,
How holy thou art,
Indestructible, too!

Rest Deep Inside

Dear Father in Heaven,

We look up to Thee
   to guide us, we pray.
We know where we're going
   but know not 'the Way,'
Save to savor each footstep
   as you direct every day.

Beloved Christ Presence,
   my buddy, my guide,
You're always there,
   already inside.
Arrows of affliction,
   flying thick and now thin;
Yet, I don't have to let them
   get under my skin.

I'll stay in pure space—
   where your impressions are clear;
I'll follow your way
   and hold you most dear
Until ascended I am
   and you offer a cheer!

The Small Inner Voice

How important it is to stop mental chatter.
The truth of all wisdom, ancient and new,
Is just to be still and listen to You.
The small inner voice, encouraged this way,
Short moments, elongated, will have their sway.

That small inner voice,
Grows, don't you see?
Becomes, strong—certain knowing
That keeps life flowing
With bliss benefit showing!

Most Dear

Wonder of wonders, awe in my soul—
With your gift of grace you've made me whole.

This journey in *mater* started so long ago.
This desire to master, this desire to know.

I've twisted and turned; I've been up and down;
I've hooked and been hooked; I've been all over town!

Yet, whene'er I looked up to rise above pain,
It's your beauty I saw and I breathed in Your Name.

Oh, many the lives and personas I've lived;
They all fall away as with your grace I am sieved.

Yes, wonder of wonders, as I sit still and clear
It is You I am touching and holding most dear.

Great Spirit I AM

Flood me with light,
    I AM Presence bright!
I'm here for You;
    what should I do?

Sent long ago and far away
    on a mission clear,
But then I forgot You are right here!
    and through time and density,
The mission's become an obscurity.

So now the conundrum
    of life in this place
Is thinking I have some other face.
    I've forgotten that You really are in me,
Forgotten that I am Your seed
    in this samsaric sea.

I am a scintilla
    of Your great solar flame,
Sent here to be and do—
    in Your Name.

All of my wanting
   and hoping to be
Is Your learning and willing
   inside of me.

When I've mastered the elements
   of this matter plane,
When I've learned and become
   all this in Your Name,
My victory is nigh—
   our home is the same.

In alchemical marriage—
   no longer amiss,
But joined as we were
   when we started all this.
Moving on through cosmos
   united in bliss!

Great Spirit,
   I am calling to Thee!
Help me remember
   each moment, each day;
I AM That I AM—
   my heart is Your clay!

Put Your Arms Around Me

O beloved Christ Presence
Thou guardian of my soul,
Put your arms around me,
As through the day I toil.

You are my rock, my guidepost,
My 'true north' of storied fame.
Without your inspiration,
I would be lost and lame.

It's with your constant blessing
As through the days we glide
Each evening is an ending—
With a smile, deep inside!

The Touchstone

Light and love flow freely from above;
   We can catch them in the air
      As they hover everywhere.

Miracles and transformations,
   Anywhere that love is spoken
      We feel their blessings unbroken.

And when we listen with our heart,
   A whispered voice to us imparts,
      this timeless Truth…

"For our time, in this abode of tears,
   The remedy is— always, already near—
      The Touchstone is Your Heartflame dear."

Magic and Grace

My life has been filled with magic and grace
It is because, in truth, I honor Pure Space.

The words I have written, here within,
I hope will give your heart a spin.

When all is said and all is done,
It's true that our life's karma is not just fun,

May your understanding emerge anew
As these butterfly kisses caress your view.

With Joy and Love,
From My Heart of Hearts,
to the Heart of the One
in You.

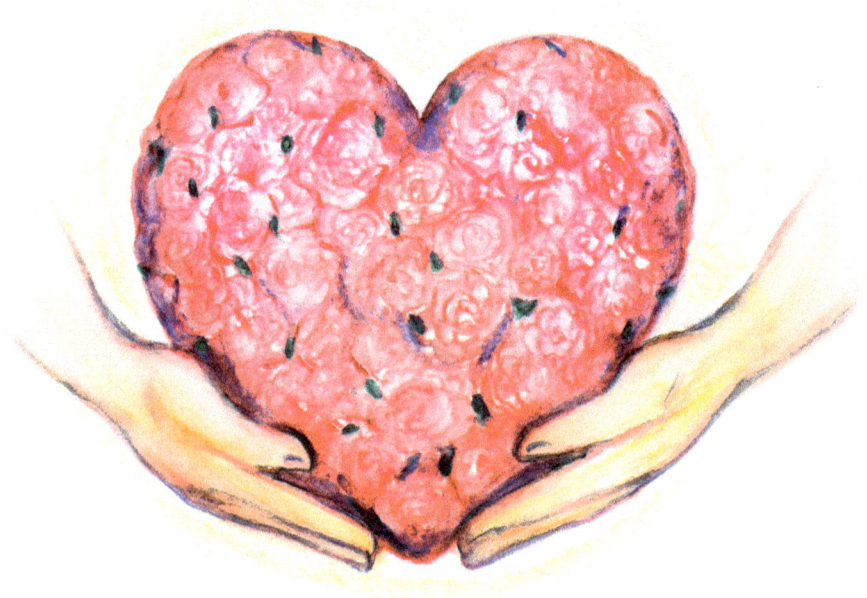

www.ingramcontent.com/pod-product-compliance
Lightning Source LLC
Chambersburg PA
CBHW061821290426
44110CB00027B/2941